STEP TO
THE MUSIC
YOU HEAR

Volume I

D0030767

Other books by

Blue Mountain Arts inc.

Come Into the Mountains, Dear Friend
by Susan Polis Schutz
I Want to Laugh, I Want to Cry
by Susan Polis Schutz
Peace Flows from the Sky
by Susan Pols Schutz

The Best Is Yet to Be
The International Grandmothers' Cookbook
Step to the Music You Hear, Vol. II
The Desiderata of Happiness
The Language of Friendship
Whatever Is, Is Best
Poor Richard's Quotations
The Language of Love

STEP TO
THE MUSIC
YOU HEAR

Volume I

Philosophical Poems from
modern and classical authors

Edited by
Susan Polis Schutz

Designed and illustrated by
Stephen Schutz

Blue
Mountain
Arts, inc.
Boulder, Colorado

This book is dedicated to James W. Ramsay

Library of Congress Catalog Card Number: 73-92895
ISBN Number: 0-88396-004-4

Manufactured in the United States of America

BLUE MOUNTAIN ARTS, INC.
P.O. Box 4549
Boulder Colorado 80302

First Printing, January, 1974
Second Printing, April, 1974
Third Printing, November, 1974
Fourth Printing, November, 1975

CONTENTS

INTRODUCTION

"Do your own thing" expresses in today's jargon an idea which is not new. It has been expressed by many generations of writers who have asserted themselves as individualists.

Step to the Music You Hear is a collection of poems on such a philosophy. William Shakespeare writes about the happy man as one "who doth ambition shun and loves to lie in the sun," and Ralph Waldo Emerson claims that "a man must be a nonconformist." But it is Henry David Thoreau who states his idea most powerfully: "Let him step to the music he hears, however measured or far away."

Susan Polis Schutz

Why should we be in such
desperate haste to succeed
and in such desperate enterprises?
If a man does not keep pace
with his companions,
perhaps it is because he hears
a different drummer.
Let him step to the music
he hears,
however measured or far away.

Henry David Thoreau

I GO MY WAY

All round is haste, confusion, noise.
For power and wealth men stretch the day
From dawn till dusk. But quietly
I go my way.

For glitter, show, to taunt the crowd,
Desire-tossed in wild dismay,
Men sell their souls. But quietly
I go my way.

The green of all the fields is mine,
The stars, the night, the wind at play,
A peaceful heart, while quietly
I go my way.

Max Ehrmann

AWAY

I weary of these noisy nights,
Of shallow jest and coarse "good cheer"
Of jazzy sounds and brilliant lights.
Come, Love, let us away from here.

Let us lay down this heavy load;
And, side by side, far from the town,
Drive on some lovely country road;
And, wondering, watch the sun go down.

What time is left to us, come, Love.
The woods, the fields shall make us whole;
The nightly pageantry above
Our little world, keeps sweet our soul.

No peace this city's madness yields —
A tawdry world in cheap veneer.
Out there the lovely woods and fields.
Come, Love, let us away from here.

Max Ehrmann

you shall above all things be glad and young.
For if you're young, whatever life you wear

it will become you; and if you are glad
whatever's living will yourself become.
Girlboys may nothing more than boygirls need:
i can entirely her only love

whose any mystery makes every man's
flesh put space on; and his mind take off time

that you should ever think, may god forbid
and (in his mercy) you true lover spare;
for that way knowledge lies, the foetal grave
called progress, and negation's dead undoom.

I'd rather learn from one bird how to sing
than teach ten thousand stars how not to dance

E. E. Cummings

Whoso would be a man,
must be a nonconformist.
He who would gather mortal
palms must not be hindered by
the name of goodness,
but must explore if it be goodness.
Nothing is at last sacred
but the integrity of your own mind.
Absolve you to yourself, and you
shall have the suffrage of the world.

Ralph Waldo Emerson

Do not follow where
the path may lead.
Go, instead, where
there is no path
and leave a trail.

Anonymous

ANIMALS

Think I could turn and live with animals,
    they are so placid and self-contained;
Stand and look at them long and long.
They do not sweat and whine about their
    condition;
They do not lie awake in the dark and weep
    for their sins;
They do not make me sick discussing their
    duty to God;
Not one is dissatisfied—not one is demented
    with the mania of owning things;
Not one kneels to another, nor to his kind
    that lived thousands of years ago;
Not one is respectable or industrious over
    the whole earth.

Walt Whitman

Far from today, tomorrow, but nay the past,
In silence, I am alone

Not knowing man nor woman, yea child,
Your tomorrow . . . I am alone

In need to be, to touch yea speak,
Oh to speak, to speak, to speak.

And to touch upon Life
with mind and mind . . .
        But to touch upon Life,
            I am alone.

Robert Polis

I went to the woods because
I wished to live deliberately,
to front only the essential
facts of life, and see if I
could not learn what it had to teach,
and not, when I came to die,
discover that I had not lived.

Henry David Thoreau

Happiness resides
not in possessions
and not in gold,
the feeling of happiness
dwells in the soul.

Democritus
420 B.C.

Happy the man, whose wish and care
A few paternal acres bound,
Content to breathe his native air
  In his own ground.

Whose herds with milk, whose fields with bread,
Whose flocks supply him with attire;
Whose trees in summer yield him shade
  In winter, fire.

Blest, who can unconcern'dly find
Hours, days, and years, slide soft away
In health of body, peace of mind,
  Quiet by day,

Sound sleep by night; study and ease
Together mixed; sweet recreation,
And innocence, which most does please
With meditation.

Thus let me live, unseen, unknown;
Thus unlamented let me die;
Steal from the world, and not a stone
  Tell where I lie.

      Alexander Pope

Do what you want to do
Be what you want to be
Look the way you want to look
Act the way you want to act

Think the way you want to think
Speak the way you want to speak
Follow the goals you want to follow

Live according to the truths within yourself

Susan Polis Schutz

Come into the mountains, dear friend
Leave society and take no one with you
But your true self
Get close to nature
Your everyday games will be insignificant
Notice the clouds spontaneously
    forming patterns
And try to do that with your life

Susan Polis Schutz

Far away there in the sunshine
are my highest aspirations. I may
not reach them, but I can look up
and see their beauty, believe in them,
and try to follow where they lead.

Louisa May Alcott

No bird soars too high,
if he soars with his own wings.

William Blake

Voyager upon life's sea,
　　To yourself be true;
And where'er your lot may be,
　　Paddle your own canoe.
Never, though the winds may rave,
　　Falter nor look back,
But upon the darkest wave
　　Leave a shining track.

Nobly dare the wildest storm,
　　Stem the hardest gale,
Brave of heart and strong of arm,
　　You will never fail.
When the world is cold and dark,
　　Keep an end in view,
And toward the beacon mark
　　Paddle your own canoe.

Every wave that bears you on
　　To the silent shore,
From its sunny source has gone
　　To return no more:
Then let not an hour's delay
　　Cheat you of your due;
But while it is called to-day,
　　Paddle your own canoe.

If your birth denied you wealth,
　　Lofty state, and power,
Honest fame and hardy health
　　Are a better dower;

But if these will not suffice,
    Golden gain pursue,
And to win the glittering prize,
    Paddle your own canoe.

Would you wrest the wreath of fame
    From the hand of Fate?
Would you write a deathless name
    With the good and great?
Would you bless your fellowmen?
    Heart and soul imbue
With the holy task, and then
    Paddle your own canoe.

Would you crush the tyrant
    Wrong,
    In the world's fierce fight?
With a spirit brave and strong,
    Battle for the Right;
And to break the chains that bind
    The many to the few—
To enfranchise slavish mind,
    Paddle your own canoe.

Nothing great is lightly won,
    Nothing won is lost—
Every good deed nobly done,
    Will repay the cost;
Leave to Heaven, in humble trust,
    All you will to do;
But if you succeed, you must
    Paddle your own canoe.

Sarah K. Bolton

Though we travel
    the world over
        to find the beautiful,
    we must carry it with us
        or we will
            find it not.

Ralph Waldo Emerson

It is easy in the world to follow the world's opinions; it is easy in solitude to follow our own; but the great man is he who in the midst of the crowd keeps with perfect sweetness the independence of solitude.

Ralph Waldo Emerson

The world is a difficult world indeed,
And the people are hard to suit,
And the man who plays on the violin
Is a bore to the man with a flute,
And I myself have often thought,
How very much better 'twould be
If every one of the folks that I know
Would only agree with me.
But since they will not, the very best way
To make the world look bright,
Is never to mind what others say,
But do what you think is right.

Light and Life Evangel

Out of the night that covers me,
  Black as the Pit from pole to pole,
I thank whatever gods may be
  For my unconquerable soul.

In the fell clutch of circumstance
  I have not winced nor cried aloud.
Under the bludgeonings of chance
  My head is bloody, but unbowed.

Beyond this place of wrath and tears
  Looms but the Horror of the shade,
And yet the menace of the years
  Finds and shall find me unafraid.

It matters not how strait the gate,
  How charged with punishments the scroll,
I am the master of my fate:
  I am the captain of my soul.

William Ernest Henley

I want to travel the common road
With the great crowd surging by,
Where there's many a laugh and many a load,
And many a smile and sigh.
I want to be on the common way
With its endless tramping feet,
In the summer bright and winter gray,
In the noonday sun and heat.
In the cool of evening with shadows nigh,
At dawn, when the sun breaks clear,
I want the great crowd passing by,
To ken what they see and hear.
I want to be one of the common herd,
Not live in a sheltered way,
Want to be thrilled, want to be stirred
By the great crowd day by day;
To glimpse the restful valleys deep,
To toil up the rugged hill,
To see the brooks which shyly creep,
To have the torrents thrill.
I want to laugh with the common man
Wherever he chance to be,
I want to aid him when I can
Whenever there's need of me.
I want to lend a helping hand
Over the rough and steep
To a child too young to understand —
To comfort those who weep.
I want to live and work and plan
With the great crowd surging by,
To mingle with the common man,
No better or worse than I.

Silas H. Perkins

I will be a man among men;
and no longer a dreamer
among shadows. Henceforth
be mine a life of action and reality!
I will work in my own sphere,
nor wish it other than it is.
This alone is health and happiness.

Henry Wadsworth Longfellow

MOUNTAIN WOMAN

I'm a mountain woman now,
Left my city ways behind,
Going to climb the highest mountain
My spirit can find.
I'm going to know these mountains,
I'll walk a trail of snow,
Going to find where the deer are hid
And where the rabbits go.

I'm a mountain woman now,
Left my city dress packed up,
Going to wear out my snowshoes
Til the summer sun comes up.
Then I'll dress my soul in beauty,
I'll wear a simple gown
With green leaves for a necklace
And flowers for a crown.

I'll search for truth and honesty,
I'll find peace of mind,
Going to find out where love is hid
Wounded by our kind.
I'm a mountain woman now
In these hills up to the sky,
O let my soul still wander
In these mountains when I die.

Shirley Schnirel

EARTH SONG

Spirit gathered
and dreamed
the billion stars
and Earth.
From Earth
Life rose,
and learned
to feel
and know and
(in a billion years
of wonderment)
to become . . .
Man.
Man
can learn
to unfurl
his soul
to sail
before the Magic . . .
to unfurl
his body,
mind and heart
in work-play,
love,
delight . . .
and soar
Earth's
rising Song
of Life.

James Meadows

IT COULDN'T BE DONE

Somebody said that it couldn't be done,
    But he with a chuckle replied
That "maybe it couldn't," but he would be one
    Who wouldn't say so till he'd tried.
So he buckled right in with the trace of a grin
    On his face. If he worried he hid it.
He started to sing as he tackled the thing
    That couldn't be done, and he did it.

Somebody scoffed: "Oh, you'll never do that;
    At least no one ever has done it";
But he took off his coat and he took off his hat,
    And the first thing we knew he'd begun it.
With a lift of his chin and a bit of a grin,
    Without any doubting or quiddit,
He started to sing as he tackled the thing
    That couldn't be done, and he did it.

There are thousands to tell you it cannot be done,
    There are thousands to prophesy failure;
There are thousands to point out to you,
        one by one,
    The dangers that wait to assail you.
But just buckle in with a bit of a grin,
    Just take off your coat and go to it;
Just start to sing as you tackle the thing
    That "cannot be done," and you'll do it.

Edgar A. Guest

One ship drives east, and another west
With the self-same winds that blow;
'Tis the set of the sails
And not the gales,
Which decides the way to go.

Like the winds of the sea are the ways of fate;
As the voyage along through life;
'Tis the will of the soul
That decides its goal,
And not the calm or the strife.

Ella Wheeler Wilcox

We must not make the past the
only light for the ensuing years.
A new leaf must be turned and
new ideas read. We must hear
things that have never been heard
before. Thus will a new world arise.

David Polis

Tell the world I'm out
I want to meditate
I want to learn who I am
and why I am here.

I want to meditate and think
about the wonders of nature
I want to be free to feel
the meaning of life.

David Polis

If you can't be a pine on the top of the hill,
    Be a scrub in the valley—but be
The best little scrub by the side of the rill;
    Be a bush if you can't be a tree.

If you can't be a bush be a bit of the grass,
    And some highway happier make;
If you can't be a muskie then just be a bass—
    But the liveliest bass in the lake!

  We can't all be captains, we've got to be crew,
    There's something for all of us here,
There's big work to do, and there's lesser to do,
    And the task you must do is the near.

If you can't be a highway then just be a trail,
    If you can't be the sun be a star;
It isn't by size that you win or you fail—
    Be the best of whatever you are!

Douglas Malloch

Isn't it strange
That princes and kings,
And clowns that caper
In sawdust rings,
And common people
Like you and me
Are builders for eternity?

Each is given a bag of tools,
A shapeless mass,
A book of rules;
And each must make —
Ere life is flown —
A stumbling block
Or a steppingstone.

R. L. Sharpe

If you want to live in the country
If you want to live in the city
If you want to be a carpenter
If you want to be an artist
Do it!

If you want to tell someone they are right
If you want to tell someone they are wrong
If you want to tell someone you are happy
If you want to tell someone you are sorry
Tell it!

Do you like to dress neat?
Do you like to dress sloppy?
Do you want to have long hair?
Do you want to have short hair?

                              Look it.

Do you want to love men?
Do you want to love women?
Do you want a lot of friends?
Do you want to be alone?

                              Do it.

If you feel like screaming
If you feel like laughing
If you feel like talking
If you feel like being silent

                              Feel it.

Do it.
Tell it.
Look it.
Feel it.
Now.
It's your only chance.
Live the life you dream
Dream the life you live.

Susan Polis Schutz

To accomplish great things
we must not only act but also dream,
not only plan but also believe

Anatole France

If one advances confidently
in the direction of his dreams,
and endeavors to live the life
which he has imagined,
he will meet with a success
unexpected in common hours.

Henry David Thoreau

HOLD FAST YOUR DREAMS

Hold fast your dreams!
Within your heart
Keep one still, secret spot
Where dreams may go,
And, sheltered so,
May thrive and grow
Where doubt and fear are not.
O keep a place apart,
Within your heart,
For little dreams to go!

Think still of lovely things that are not true.
Let wish and magic work at will in you.
Be sometimes blind to sorrow. Make believe!
Forget the calm that lies
In disillusioned eyes.
Though we all know that we must die,
Yet you and I
May walk like gods and be
Even now at home in immortality.

We see so many ugly things—
Deceits and wrongs and quarrelings;
We know, alas! we know
How quickly fade
The color in the west,
The bloom upon the flower,
The bloom upon the breast
And youth's blind hour.
Yet keep within your heart
A place apart
Where little dreams may go,
May thrive and grow.
Hold fast—hold fast your dreams!

Louise Driscoll

THE CRY OF A DREAMER

I am tired of planning and toiling
  In the crowded hives of men;
Heart-weary of building and spoiling,
  And spoiling and building again.
And I long for the dear old river,
  Where I dreamed my youth away;
For a dreamer lives forever,
  And a toiler dies in a day.

I am sick of the showy seeming
  Of a life that is half a lie;
Of the faces lined with scheming
  In the throng that hurries by.
From the sleepless thoughts' endeavor,
  I would go where the children play;
For a dreamer lives forever,
  And a thinker dies in a day.

I can feel no pride, but pity
  For the burdens the rich endure;
There is nothing sweet in the city
  But the patient lives of the poor.

Oh, the little hands too skillful
  And the child mind choked with weeds!
The daughter's heart grown willful,
  And the father's heart that bleeds!

No, no! from the street's rude bustle,
  From trophies of mart and stage,
I would fly to the woods' low rustle
  And the meadow's kindly page.
Let me dream as of old by the river,
  And be loved for the dream alway;
For a dreamer lives forever,
  And a toiler dies in a day.

John Boyle O'Reilly

Somewhere, there's a world to cling to
Somewhere, there's a song to sing to
Somewhere there is laughter
Somewhere there is truth
Somewhere there is happiness
Somewhere . . . .

Somewhere, there's a life worth living for
Somewhere, there's a man worth giving for
Somewhere there is hope
Somewhere there is a dream
Somewhere there is love
Somewhere . . . .

Rhonda-Lea Reid

I do not know what I may appear to the world, but to myself I seem to have been only like a boy playing on the seashore, and diverting myself in now and then finding a prettier shell or a smoother pebble than ordinary whilst the great ocean of truth lay all undiscovered before me.

Isaac Newton

Must we always teach our children
with books?
Let them look at the mountains and the stars
up above. Let them look at the beauty of
the waters and the trees and flowers on earth.
They will then begin to think, and
to think is the beginning of a real education.

David Polis

Lord, who am I to teach the way
To little children day by day,
So prone myself to go astray?

I teach them Knowledge, but I know
How faint they flicker and how low
The candles of my knowledge glow.

I teach them Power to will and do,
But only now to learn anew
My own great weakness through and through.

I teach them Love for all mankind
And all God's creatures, but I find
My love comes lagging far behind.

Lord, if their guide I still must be,
Oh, let the little children see
The teacher leaning hard on Thee.

Leslie Pinckney Hill

Life is like music; it must be composed by ear, feeling and instinct, not by rule.

Samuel Butler

Under the greenwood tree,
Who loves to lie with me,
And turn his merry note
Unto the sweet bird's throat.

Who doth ambition shun
And loves to lie in the sun,
Seeking the food he eats
And pleased with what he gets,
Come hither, come hither, come hither;

Here shall he see
No enemy
But winter and rough weather.

William Shakespeare

Not everything is good because it is old,
nor poems always bad by being new.
Good men try both before they
make their choice, while the fool
but takes the view of others.

Ancient Sanskrit Poem

Look to this day
for it is life
the very life of life
In its brief course lie all
the realities and truths of existence
the joy of growth
the splendor of action
the glory of power
For yesterday is but a memory
And tomorrow is only a vision
But today well lived
makes every yesterday a memory
                    of happiness
and every tomorrow a vision of hope
Look well, therefore, to this day!

Ancient Sanskrit Poem

There's music in the sighing of a reed:
There's music in the gushing of a rill;
There's music in all things, if man had ears;
The earth is but the music of the sphere.

Lord Byron

Sounds of the wind
sounds of the sea
make one happy
just to be

June Polis

BARTER

Life has loveliness to sell,
  All beautiful and splendid things,
Blue waves whitened on a cliff,
  Soaring fire that sways and sings,
And children's faces looking up
Holding wonder like a cup.

Life has loveliness to sell,
  Music like a curve of gold,
Scent of pine trees in the rain,
  Eyes that love you, arms that hold,
And for your spirit's still delight,
Holy thoughts that star the night.

Spend all you have for loveliness,
  Buy it and never count the cost;
For one white singing hour of peace
  Count many a year of strife well lost,
And for a breath of ecstasy
Give all you have been, or could be.

Sara Teasdale

ACKNOWLEDGMENTS

We gratefully acknowledge the permission granted by the following authors, publishers, and authors' representatives to reprint poems from their publications. Recognition is also made to poets and original publishers for the use of many poems which are now in the public domain.

Macmillan Publishing Co. Inc. for "Barter" from *Collected Poems of Sara Teasdale*, copyright 1917 by Macmillan Publishing Co. Inc., renewed 1945 by Mamie P. Wheless. Reprinted with permission of Macmillan Publishing Co. Inc.

Crescendo Publishing Co. for "I Go My Way" and "Away" from *The Poems of Max Ehrmann,* Copyright 1948 by Bertha K. Ehrmann. All rights reserved. Reprinted by permission of Crescendo Publishing Co. Boston.

Harcourt Brace Jovanovich Inc for "for you shall above all things be glad and young" from *Complete Poems 1913-1962 by E. E. Cummings*, Copyright 1938 by E. E. Cummings; renewed 1966 by Marion Morehouse Cummings. Reprinted with permission of Harcourt Brace Jovanovich.

Rand McNally & Co., Conkey Division, for "The Winds of Fate" by Ella Wheeler Wilcox.

Doubleday for "Hold Fast Your Dreams," from *Best Loved Poems of the American People*, by Louise Driscoll.

E.P. Dutton & Co. for "The Cry of the Dreamer" from *Moondyne* by John Boyle O'Reilly.

Doubleday for "The Common Road" from *Best Loved Poems of the American People*, by Silas Perkins.

McClure Newspaper Syndicate for "Be the Best of Whatever You Are," by Douglas Malloch. Copyright 1925 McClure Newspaper Syndicate.

Reilly & Lee Co. for "It couldn't be done" from the *Collected Verse* by Edgar Guest, Copyright 1934, by Edgar Guest. Reprinted by permission of Reilly & Lee, a division of the Henry Regnery Co., Chicago, Illinois.

A careful effort has been made to trace the ownership of poems used in this anthology in order to get permission to reprint copyright poems and to give proper credit to the copyright owners.

If any error or omission has occurred, it is completely inadvertent, and we would like to correct it in future editions provided that written notification is made to the publisher, BLUE MOUNTAIN ARTS, INC., P.O. Box 4549, Boulder, Colorado 80302.

STEP TO THE MUSIC YOU HEAR
Volume II

In the first two printings of this book we announced that everyone was welcome to submit poems for possible inclusion in a forthcoming *Volume II*. We would like to thank our readers for the wonderful response to our request. *Step to the Music You Hear, Vol. II* has now been published and consists in part of a selection of these poems.